Garden of Verses

Tahir Ali Kamil

Preface

I have had the pleasure of presenting this voluminous work to those who have been readers of my books. This anthology is a particular form of a poem with fixed rhymes.

The structure is self-explanatory, and need not be explained. One can see they are mostly intelligently structured. The first, second and third lines are in the same metre. The third line is usually a message. It may be in prose or poetry both. More often than not the third and the fourth line feed or supported by each other.

How you got to be who you are

We need not be called to be the bar

It only suffices to be right in the head

To conclude we got to be who we are

$\mathfrak{W}$hat is fated to be yours is yours

Friend to enemy, not friend to yours

Do not make friends with mean persons

They are neither yours nor ours

$\mathfrak{W}$e are worthy in every sense

What we do know is immense

We are irrevocably a masterpiece

Secrets lie behind our lens

$\mathfrak{I}$ am not reliant on you

I will do it what I do

You may do it what you do

If you feel not ashamed of you

Keep control over your temper

Refrain from anxiety and anger

Cut connections with ignorant people

I wonder if you commit a blunder

Crisis is not alone a danger

We fain call it not a danger

It is not possible to tell the whole truth

Find the blessings without anger

We tell lies for all sorts of reasons

Though not suitable for any of the seasons

It is the truth and nothing but the truth

Do not betray by way of treasons

He had fired a shot in anger

People did not call him danger

Because he is known as pious

Piety always saves in danger

Although we are the salt of the water

Do not we care to prove our worth

Humans are not created for naught

We while our time ever in mirth

Don't get lost in the crowd

If you are kind, do not be loud

It is justifiable, glorious pride

Then you are worthy to be proud

$\mathfrak{S}$un is a giver of life and heat

In praise of it drums are beat

To get the benefit of sunshine

Ways and demands, should we meet

$$\mathfrak{H}\text{e deserves to be harshly met}$$

Not to forgive or forget

He is burden on the earth

I learned the lesson to not forget

We have seen time and again

Without efforts nothing we gain

To err is human, to forgive is divine

Moral values must we retain

As you are always on the go

See the result, behold and lo!

It should come as no surprise

Do not weep, it had to be so

An error causes defeat and fall

Though it may look little and small

Do not put off annoying issue

Which must be tackled once for all

We would have to balk

And doff the offer of a talk

We have agreed to a truce

It is our choice to run or walk

$\mathfrak{I}$f you are not eccentric and odd

Have the courage to defy the odd

You are the one whose opinion is head

Why do not you rely on God?

We are going to be a light

Would we shine we are bright

We should make sincere efforts

To keep us a bit of all right

We must resist to any fear

Do not let it to come near

Habits are tough to break

Fear itself we have to fear

Courage is resistance to fear

Mastery of fear, not absence of fear

That is what Mark Twain has said

Embody courage to split and tear

$\mathfrak{L}$isten to me if you believe in me

That should be, what you are going to be

What is fated, I have to accept

Whatever the future holds for me

$\mathfrak{T}$hat is not good what you wanted

Do not take it for granted

Be content on what you have

May God lead to what he wanted

$\mathfrak{A}$ friend in need

Is a friend indeed

If he is a true friend

I am delighted indeed

Do not be afraid of

Not either you loaf

Make friends with people

We should not be off

When one is at peace with oneself

He who gives courage to himself

I don't bother who is who

It is me with identity of myself

I have got to get started

Benevolent to be I wanted

What they sow they will reap

Let them try to have thwarted

$\mathfrak{I}$ will have to carry the load

To carry out the will of god

In doing so I please you all

I agree upon I on the nod

We will have to have the courage

To satisfy demands of heroic age

Do not look dejected and sad

Heroes have a cheerful image

$\mathfrak{L}$isten please to the warning shout

Feel not dizzy thinking about

The time has now come for action

Waste not time thinking about

$\mathfrak{W}$hat was I born to do

What should I do and not do

Ignorance is great poverty

I did know it when I grew

We ought to be ashamed of

To be rather a bit off

It would be a sign of respect

If you take your hat off

$\mathfrak{D}$o not insist and bow

Facts are dragged in tow

Blessings are in disguise

Secrets thereof should we know

Though I feel not lonely ever

I will never ask a favor

Reading though has become a vice

People call me foolish never

Success lies ahead of you

Get it done which has to do

Grab the opportunity waste it not

Lest it turns its back on you

Worry thwarts not destiny

Doubt is crueler than reality

Act with destination in mind

Adversity is an opportunity

Be master in the art of listening

It is the best form of flattering

Govern yourself to govern others

Learn the value of compromising

𝕴f it is worthy to be doing

You can make it worth doing

We ought to be self-confident

Good qualities need to be nurturing

Go to bed in late evening

Get up early in the morning

It makes a man healthy, wealthy and wise

Laws of nature must be abiding

$\mathfrak{I}$f you please have your say

You will shine and send a ray

People will not call you a coward

If you have the courage to say

We know for sure it is a sign

Pertains to thine not to mine

Benefits of which go much deeper

Reason is lost in mists of time

What I say you have to lay

Do not say me nor or nay

Let it be what it may

Better put it in a bay

$\mathfrak{B}$e the light which you seek

Spirit is willing flesh is weak

No wealth is greater than wisdom

A bold man however cannot be weak

Do not be addicted to work

Work always like clockwork

Workaholism is bad to you

Why do not you seek a perk?

$\mathfrak{M}$ake a start if addicted to work

Do it however like clockwork

That is the only way to happiness

Do it no matter with a jerk

Work is love and devotion both

Shun the ills of laziness and sloth

Have had patience and forbearance

It is the work and worship both

Money has demands aside

Survival and social demands beside

Come what might it must be settled

Have it confirmed get to abide

Do I have to remind

If you do not mind

You had to find a cure

Get busy and find

After a moment's reflection

We may shun the temptation

Do it what you have to do

If you do not then you shun

We have taken care of you

You may do it what you do

It will stand you in good stead

You will get destined for you

Do careful planning if you are wise

A futile exercise to do otherwise

Planning for success is much for sure

To do otherwise is not wise

Quick decision must not be made

It may put us into the shade

Exceptions are not the rule

Right decision must be made

Judge not a person by his manners

He hides his face under layers

The more sophisticated a man is

The more his identity is of betrayers

$\mathfrak{A}$ gift we receive gives us joy

To be happy as a child with toy

It does away with even enmity

Return more to express joy

Life is the movement forward

If stands still, is going backward

Stagnation is taken for death

Salvation is moving upward

$\mathfrak{I}$f you are neighbor of a neighbor

For god's sake be a good neighbor

Prejudice springs from ignorance

If not social you have to be a beggar

We like it not but have to do

An obligation to fulfil to

There is no excuse had we if any

Do it as you are compelled to

Never, never, give up trying

To meet the goal you must be striving

We have to struggle towards attainment

Truth need not emphasizing

To stay healthy do more exercise

Go to bed early to rise

Shun anxiety, anger and worry

Take a balanced meal if you are wise

$\mathfrak{B}$orrowing devours tranquility

Whenever it comes to morality

Borrowers and lenders both are losers

They weep on their stupidity

If you shift to a foreign land

Do not be cut off do not tend

You are not a son of the soil

Adhere to your culture, language and land

Pull yourself together

Do not cause a weather

Do not have to hold aloof

You have to get together

$\mathfrak{B}$etter it is to get ahead

To get richer is however bad

To narrow gap between rich and poor

Ill-gotten wealth must not be made

$\mathfrak{B}$etter than cure is prevention

It captures no doubt our attention

It is the domain of municipality

To cause is lack of health education

Stay at a place wisely

Consult and think over widely

Rolling-stone gathers no moss

Think it well over wisely

To save money for rainy days

Saves our life in many ways

When worse situation is lying ahead

We may be forced to face the bays

Try again we are not a few

Gather courage to start anew

Defeat is a blessing of sorts

Never is it a bitter brew

Habits are though tough to break

Must we break it as a good cake

Only to have had a desired effect

Train yourself before you bake

We are meant to wait for time

Go slowly all the time

Time and tide wait for no man

That is not for yours or mine

Nurture yourself with nature

For mental health and nurture

Set up good environment

Promote goodwill and favor

You are better what you are, so do I am what I am

I do agree that is that, you may take me as I am

Greed dulls the faculties of judgment and wisdom

He is very submissive, keeps my orders, he is tame

Success demands great application

No wasteful efforts of duplication

You are amongst those who are nearer to
God

When you kneel in supplication

Have you ever thought

I care of you a lot

We ought to continue efforts

We need to do a lot

$\mathfrak{I}$ warn you over and over

Tell the driver to go slower

In order to guard your secret

You have to speak a bit lower

$So agog am I at the news

Though it was your private views

Concealed talents benefit no one

We are all agog to your views

$\mathfrak{K}$eep quiet and lull

To ponder over or mull

Be ready for the worst

Have the courage make it null

Why it gets you such a bore

We should learn it as a lore

He is not a common man

He is hero at his core

Would you listen to what I told

Would have you thought I was so bold

Certainty is not certain

A blind is a guide, lo and behold

I had had a nasty fall

That is why I had to call

We ponder over and worry about

As you are, so are we all

$\mathfrak{I}$ hold firm to my belief

It is not beyond belief

Seeing all you safe and sound

I heave a sigh of relief

$\mathfrak{I}$f it is not worth your while

Why do not you make your pile

The burden of grief is hard to bear

You may repose for a while

If you help the poor and needy

God responds when you are needy

You ruined the health being greedy

I shall pray to recover speedy

Why they believe what they believe

Let me do it what I believe

Bear it whatever befalls you

Emotions, by weeping, you may relieve

Did you ever get to know?

We are born not high or low

We should get along with people

You will reap it what you sow

We are not above the law

So we do not break the law

There is a wolf in sheep's clothing

Do not believe in what you saw

Do not you see

Who would it be

Either of us will have to suffer

Either you or me

Why do not we get going

Seeds of virtue we must be sowing

Do not make polluting noise

We should not always be rowing

What you want to be like

Your manners are childlike

You are supposed to be wise

Behave towards all alike

Afraid not of your own shadow

So far alone we can go

In the face of fear and hatred

Above and beyond we will go

He has been the vagabond so the story runs

We are on standby whatever happens

Pious man does not fall, pray or evil doers

To save his piety; he keeps away and shuns

𝕴f you do not want to follow

It is time to unfollow

You have only today to do it

You will never see tomorrow

It is more than to meets the eye

Why to ask you who am I

Why on earth I should ask

I will go to where and why

Your behavior is indecent

You should follow what I meant

If you do not follow me

Follow please your own bent

$\mathfrak{I}$f we are feeling a bit below par

It may spoil our career and mar

We have gotten so far to do

We have the right to be who we are

Obligation is enough to blind

Still do not you mind

It leaves lots to be desired

Because love is blind

$\mathfrak{I}$ am not taking of your nagging

It is of your own making

Summon your courage for the battle

Have the strength you are lacking

Certainty is not certain

Does not disorder contain

Wise man may be a fool

This rule here does not pertain

$\mathfrak{L}$earned man may not be wise

Do not guess what is his size

We must follow the maxim

Go to bed early, early to rise

Have in your body two of me

Live with just one of me

Hold firm to your beliefs

That is what it would be

$\mathfrak{I}$ need not hear the ways and wherefores

When it comes from reliable source

He implored and I pardoned him

The culprit knelt on all his fours

You can speak to your heart's desire

Hitherto you do not seem to tire

It is a situation wheels within wheels

A lawyer they say is a liar

We make fears allay

Despite what they say

To keep our future safe

We have to kill or cure

Pious persons hold piety

They are to serve humanity

Wealth is a product of greed

Good men serve the cause of humanity

𝕴 do not you let you alone

I will make you feel at home

Be not depressed brooding over

To be bygone, be bygone

$\mathfrak{I}$f you make a lot of pile

That is hardly worth your while

Merrymaking is agreeable

If you do it once in a while

Your attitude is to be holier than thou

But we know better what you are now

Be wiser to be humble and meek

They do not regard you as a sacred cow

You are worthy to hold your head high

What you have said should not be a lie

When I heard you were safe

To my great relief I heaved a sigh

We take it with a pinch of salt

You can tell me what you want

Though he does not seem to care

What you like you can rant

$\mathfrak{A}$lthough beyond our power and remit

We may do it bit by bit

We often exclaim such a thing

That is a cry of joy we emit

$\mathfrak{Y}$ou can all you like rant and rave

Keep the fool away from himself, to save

To create a situation

We have the way to pave

$\mathfrak{M}$uch to my chagrin and to avoid disgrace

I get itchy feet and move from place to place

Let it be so, I do not care

If defeat is staring me in the face

Wounds and wisdom teach you well

Enhance wellbeing where you dwell

Do away with acute grief

Embrace hugging, and get well

You are the man who care for you

He is no one other than you

Take the world as it comes

You are wise, you can woo

$\mathfrak{I}$ got started for the cause

How sad and bad and mad it was

I had to leave my comfort zone

You called me later great I was

$\mathfrak{F}$ocus on journey not the goal

Joy is in doing heart and soul

Capture your attention on peace of mind

Be not selfish, filthy and foul

How to do it, what do I do

Teach yourself how do you do

I am sorry one of the people

Do not bother what do I do

Let me do it what I do

Ask me never am I who

Be a hero in field of battle

That is just worthwhile too

$\mathfrak{D}$o not unsay what you say

If you have the courage to say

Every truth is not to be told

Keep it lying in a bay

𝕷et our love to each other share

Though your love is beyond compare

Choose the star I made for you

That will give you hope and care

To come to know who you are

Step on, you are not very far

Put on the cart before the horse

It would your career make or mar

You should do it what I do

Like for others you like for you

Take rough also with the smooth

This you keep in mind too

Ｉf we have a preternatural ability

We are the master of our destiny

Life is not an empty dream

It is a twist of fail that controls our destiny

$\mathfrak{L}$et it happen when it happens

We do not know why it happens

Love those who love you

These are our only weapons

$\mathfrak{L}$et him who will believe

Let him also who will disbelieve

If a misfortune befalls

Ask God to relieve

Do not lie a monstrous lie

You are better to be a shy

Cautious people do not err

Once bitten twice shy

Ⱨe worked till he was blue in the face

But he could not win the race

It had not had a marked effect

Because the motive was man and base

Let us have some peace

To get back in one piece

Actions speak louder than words

Do not ever cheat and fleece

$\mathfrak{B}$ehave well be just to all

Be kind but trust not all

Do not blow your own trumpet

You are a fool if going to fall

If you listen to what I say

Then comply with and obey

See not any perfection

True love finds ever a way

Present is not to be the last

It is the product of the past

Do not forget past achievements

Be wise learning of the past

You will lose the treasure bore

If you do not thereof care

Lose not hope in god's mercy

Cautious people seldom err

Due to beliefs, which I abide

All my fears are laid aside

Who has character, has the courage

On perseverance I have to reside

Think it twice before you speak

Better is it than climb to a peak

Patience is a kind of bravery

Be wise to be humble and meek

$\mathfrak{A}$s we stay on good terms

Need not stiffen with gums

Do not choose a ride of

A roller coaster of emotions

Avoid disgrace and save your face

If you regard for others, it is an ideal base

Have deep, sincere respect for others

It is not commendable if motives are base

$\mathfrak{M}$y home is sacred as a shrine

In profound darkness does it shine

East or west, home is the best

Home is the best, so it is mine

$\mathfrak{G}$et it done with unbated zeal

A devout wish you deeply feel

Let not trivia bother you

Do not hide what you feel

$\mathfrak{F}$eed your mind with beauty

Learning is your duty

Be nice to others

Do in the line of duty

Whenever I get near my goal

I try to do it with heart and soul

Nothing succeeds like success

So, I succeeded to get my goal

Things are not working right

So, we have to get it right

Although we could lie in comfort

Even though we have to fight

There is a process to be a creator

The creative process to be an inventor

You have not hard nut to crack

You have the wisdom to be an orator

Powerful is the action in time

Although it is not worth a dime

Although people like to relish

But it is as sour as a lime

Open yourself to enjoy blessings

To fly with they are the wings

Measure the effect of your action

You will possess all great things

$\mathfrak{W}$hat we save is what we earn

From the bees and ants, we learn

Be wiser in the living present

Bygone days do not return

Success is akin to hard work

Cannot it be due to sheer luck

There are reasons behind it

If success comes without work

We are because all they are

That is why we are at par

Do it sooner if you can

Do not dwell on what you are

If you have got to get a sleep

Fruits of which will you heap

Honest people look in the face

Going astray going to weep

$\mathfrak{L}$et us do some cleaning too

If you do not, let me do

Lust and greed have no limit

Lose not sight of this too

Get there to get there

That is not a joke mere

It takes courage to fulfil a dream

Cost of which you have to bear

$\mathfrak{I}$f you have the will to fight

Rise then to your full height

To be above most others

Sow the strength of will and might

$\mathfrak{L}$ife is that, that is life

Everywhere crime is rife

If you dislike me

Do not please twist the knife

How to behave, let it be known

You will reap what you have sown

Do not weep over spilt milk

Let bygone, be bygone

If you love to eat, nothing but loaf

I am afraid, you may be called an oaf

There may be something up

You are rather a bit off

$\mathfrak{T}$o see you have not seen

Wipe the slate clean

To make a fresh start

You must find a mean

Culprit you are in the name of the law

Though it was so wrong what I saw

It could have been better than it is

If had not shown life in the raw

$\mathfrak{I}$f the cat is out of the bag

Do not complain, criticize and nag

Do it as soon as you can

We cannot afford further a lag

We have always been at pains

Like the prisoners kept in chains

Make hay while the sun shines

Do not do it when it rains

$\mathfrak{A}$re you not going to wake?

Future there is at stake

Let it befall what it may

Which you have to undertake

$\mathfrak{W}$hat is it that makes me wiser?

Why do people call me wiser?

Hoard it never for its own sake

Do not let them call you miser

$$\mathfrak{H}$$ow to do it, what I do

Teach yourself how do you do

I am only one of the people

Do not bother what do I do

After dinner walk a mile

After lunch repose a while

It has been judgment of elders

Act upon is worth your while

Do not defer to be wise

Mix not truths with the lies

When to take a bold decision

Look straight in the eyes

$\mathfrak{L}$et the beauty shine through

As it looks great on you

Our legacy lives forever

They will forget who were you

Never delay to launch the strife

Do it while the time is ripe

When the iron is quite hot

Then only we have to strike

It is a dream which he dreams

That is beyond my wildest dreams

It is not by chance which i came across

I do not dream impossible dreams

$\mathfrak{W}$hile you need not my pressure

What you say makes no sense

Though it is not obligatory

I shall oblige your presence

$\mathfrak{W}$hile I want to put you right

Why should you keep out of sight

We do not intend to hound you out

Do not go in the dead of night

He does not care a fuck about

We have therefore no need to shout

To be sure you are the winner

As for you there is no room for doubt

Do not shed crocodile tears

You cannot be sheep away among the bears

Despite she knows the whole truth

It is the blame that she bears

You are the person in the know

They are not just for show

Athough it is not for sale

You may keep it even though

Believe me I do not intend to cheat

I only want just demands to meet

Do not either hurry or worry

You need to rest as you look dead beat

Two wrongs do not make a right

If you are right, why do not you fight

You need not be in the doldrums

I support your cause with all my might

Vocabulary

mirth = joy, happiness, laughter

naught (also nought) = nothing

> His efforts came to naught (were
> unsuccessful)

doff = to take one's hat off

don = to put on clothes etc.

balk = (also baulk) to be unwilling to do
something because of dangers etc.;

> to block somebody's plans
> deliberately

loaf = to waste time doing nothing

to be off = not to be polite or friendly with somebody

thwart = to present somebody, doing what he intends to do;

      to oppose a plan successfully

nod = to show agreement and say "yes"

      moving head down and up quickly

mist = a thin fog: The originals of the story are lost in the mists of time

to be like clockwork = smoothly, according to plan

jerk = a quick, sudden, sharp movement: The bus stopped with a jerk

remit = the area which is in one's control and influence

rant = to speak loudly and angrily for a long time against injustice

to take something with a pinch of salt = not to take seriously

the apple of one's eye = a loved one, precious person

preternatural = beyond what is natural and normal

oaf = a stupid, awkward person

to have / get itchy feet = to feel a desire to travel from place to place